LEVERAGE
FEAR
AND
ACHIEVE
SUCCESS

Also written by Shanna McFarlane

Profit in Any Market with Real Estate Investing

18 Months to Wealth with Real Estate Investing

Homeless on the Street to Owning the Street

LEVERAGE FEAR AND ACHIEVE SUCCESS

Six Powerful Steps in Using Fear to Your Advantage

Shanna McFarlane

iUniverse, Inc.
Bloomington

LEVERAGE FEAR AND ACHIEVE SUCCESS
SIX POWERFUL STEPS IN USING FEAR TO YOUR ADVANTAGE

iUniverse books may be ordered through booksellers or by contacting:

iUniverse
1663 Liberty Drive
Bloomington, IN 47403
www.iuniverse.com
1-800-Authors (1-800-288-4677)

ISBN: 978-1-4620-4611-9 (sc)
ISBN: 978-1-4620-4612-6 (hc)
ISBN: 978-1-4620-4614-0 (ebk)

Library of Congress Control Number: 2011914374

Printed in the United States of America

iUniverse rev. date: 08/17/2011

Contents

Chapter Seven

To my mother and grandmother,

Elaine and Inez Lawood

Mommy—Thank you for always being strong all those years ago and for making all the sacrifices you made for us. You taught me how to be resilient, not to give up, and how to face and overcome any obstacle.

Mama—Thank you for teaching me to believe in myself, regardless of what anyone else thought of me. Thank you for seeing me for who I truly am and for encouraging me to always let my light shine on the world.

Preface

I've written this book for the millions of men, women, and children who spend their best years or even a lifetime being paralyzed by the emotion known as fear.

They spend their time worrying about many things that may never happen, having panic attacks and choosing to remain still instead of moving forward. I have been fortunate; through my experiences, I have come to realize that this emotion that we often fight to overcome can actually be leveraged and used to our advantage.

In life, we are faced with many challenges on a daily basis, some harder to overcome than others. Fear of failure, fear of rejection, fear of change, fear of losing someone, and even fear of success have caused many great minds to go to waste and many talents to stay untouched. Our limiting beliefs about the things we are capable of and the fear of failing have stopped many of us short of achieving our vision.

We must learn *not* to be crippled by fear, but to use fear to our advantage and step forward into our greatness through faith. We must change the way we view fear and our relationship with it in order to see it as a form of motivation.

Seeing my mother struggle the way she did when I was a child not only broke my heart but also built my character and gave me the tenacity to go after more for myself. Because of my fear of the living a similar life, I fought hard to become much more.

There were nights I lay in bed watching my mother try to contain her tears after I'd come home from school and handed her a note from my teacher advising her she needed to purchase my textbooks or I would be suspended from school. She tried hard not to let us hear or see her vulnerable. She would cry until she fell asleep. Even though she couldn't afford it, she wanted us to have the best education possible. I can only imagine a fraction of the turmoil she went through fighting her way through each day.

After experiencing the struggles she went through "up close and personal," one of my biggest fears was to grow up and live the difficult life my mother lived, unable to provide for my children the way I wanted to and unable to provide them with what they deserved to have.

As I was growing up, just the thought of this happening scared me into developing a resilient mind-set, dreaming big, planning strategically, taking action, identifying opportunities, falling and bouncing back, creating my own path if one didn't exist, working "right" and working "smart," and exploring avenues I probably wouldn't have explored.

Sharing my experiences with you is my gift to you to remind you that fear can be leveraged and used to your advantage. Instead of allowing myself to be paralyzed by fear, I've embraced it and applied it to all areas of my life; by doing so, I was able to achieve a high level of success. These experiences will illustrate how you, too, can do so.

This book is based on my real-life experiences. I will show you how to determine whether or not your fear is a healthy one—whether it is an "essential" or a "non-essential" fear—and how to use it or reduce it, regardless of what it is.

You can expect the things outlined in this book to be life-changing. Most of it will warm your heart, and most importantly, this book will change your thoughts and your perception of things. By following the steps outlined, you will understand how "fear," one of the biggest emotions that exist, can change and improve your life immensely. By applying the steps, you will find yourself achieving success in all the things you had given up on, things like your aspirations, your dreams, your vision, your relationships, and your very life!

To reap the full benefits of the information provided in this book, you must keep an open mind and view things objectively. Remember it was written with you in mind; my intention is to pass on invaluable knowledge I have gained through life-changing experiences.

Don't allow your fear of learning something new to stop you short of achieving something great. That is exactly what this book is designed to do for you—to provide you with the knowledge and the straightforward call-to-action steps that will improve your life to greatness!

This book was intentionally written as a summary, short and to the point.

To help you solidify what you've learnt throughout this book, I have included "Call to Action" sections in each chapter. In these sections, I provide you with examples and the right tools to enable you to apply what you've learned to your own unique situation. I've included notebook pages for you to write your responses. This serves as a great learning tool.

Let this be one of the books you carry with you at all times, whether in your laptop case or your purse or your lunch pack. Fear is always lurking around somewhere, and in the event you need a reminder, you can easily refer back to the information in the book or the "Call to Action" section you completed.

My eleven-year-old daughter Tyra has contributed to this preface with a real-life experience in which she had to make a decision to fight back when fear played a role in a decision she was about to make in a situation at school. See her contribution below. Tyra's experience is included to remind you that on a daily basis our children are confronted with the same emotions and insecurities we face as adults. We must teach our children at an early age how to use their fear in the right context, leveraging it successfully and using it to their advantage. Remember, our children are the future generation of leaders.

The bottom is too crowded, so I'll see you at the top.

To Your Success!

Shanna

A Child's Experience with Fear

My name is Tyra. I am 11 years old. Just a couple of months ago my teacher assigned a project; we had to create a product that kids our age would buy. Initially I choose to work by myself. I was confident I could produce something great that I would be proud of, something that would demonstrate my capabilities to my class. Even though I knew I could complete this successfully, I was afraid of failing. Because of my fear of failure and my lack of confidence in myself, I took the easy way out; I decided to ask my friends if I could join their group.

When I explained my situation and my decision to my mom, she gave me a new perspective to deal with the fear I was feeling. I realized that fear was taking control of me mentally and emotionally, so

I decided to try my best to be strong and think of what I would miss if I went against what I really wanted. Even though I was still afraid of failing, deep within me I knew I really wanted to complete the project alone, as I knew I had something unique to contribute. In the long run, I was more afraid of being unhappy with my decision, giving up on an opportunity I may not have again, and having to live with the consequences.

I made the decision to do the project alone and give it my best.

The project was completed and I got an amazing mark. My teacher and my classmates were very surprised at how well I carried my own.

I have learned from that experience that we can't let fear take over our lives. Sometimes we may need to talk with someone about our fears to keep us from making a mistake or not taking a chance on ourselves. I also learned that I was more afraid of what I would miss out on if I didn't give myself a chance by completing the project on my own. This decision made all the difference in the world!

Say no to fear of the wrong things!

Tyra Forbes

Fear exists whether we care to admit it or not. If its existence is beyond our control, we must live with it. If we must live with it, why not have it work *for us* instead of against us?

Acknowledgments

To the best girl in the world, my beautiful daughter, Tyra Forbes. Thank you for agreeing to co-write the preface to this book; you did an amazing job. Thank you for your belief in your mom's dream and all your support in making this book a success. Most importantly, thank you for being you and always saying, "Mom, I know you can do it."

I have the best daughter in the world!

To the special men in my life, the "Forbes gentlemen," my husband, Mark, and my son, MJ. You guys rock! Thank you for being understanding and supportive of my journey. Thanks for cheering me on from the sidelines. You make it easier than it could have been. Thank you for being a part of my life and in my corner.

You guys are a blessing!

To my dear friend Semone Palmer. Where do I begin? Words cannot describe my gratitude. I could not have done this without you cheering me on; your unwavering support and your thoughtfulness and kind words have been invaluable. You believed in me even on the days I didn't believe in myself. Thank you for all the support you've given me. Thank you for being my friend, for holding me accountable, for reminding me how talented I truly am, and most important, for giving me the courage to pursue my passion and share my story with the world in the hope of making a difference and improving someone's life.

I am so blessed to have you in my life!

Shanz

Most importantly, I would like to thank God for his many blessings and for shining his light in my life, so that I can be an example to the world.

Thank you for every step, for every obstacle, for every opportunity, for every success, for the entire journey, and most important, for choosing my life to be an inspiration to others.

I am truly blessed!

Thank you to my family and friends and to everyone that contributed to my journey!

Much Love!

Shanna

Chapter One

The Real Truth about Fear

If you know the combination to a lock . . . it doesn't matter who you are . . . it has to open for you.

—Author Unknown

The Lost Pencil

Grade school, grade five, Mrs. B's class. Erica, a classmate of mine, had a bone to pick with me—not just that day, but almost every day, unless I hid at the back of the school until I was certain she had left for home.

It all started when she asked to borrow my pencil for the second time. The first time I had lent her a pencil, she had lost it and refused to help me look for it. Later that day, I got in trouble with Mrs. B for being a nuisance to another classmate from whom I had to borrow a pencil.

So it was an easy decision when she asked the second time. My response was, "No, I can't."

That clearly was not the response she expected. She whispered to me, "You'll pay for this after school." She was not joking when she said this; that very evening after school, just after we left the school premises, she approached me with such force, I was on the ground before I could even realize what was happening.

Almost every day after school, she would pick a fight and pretty much beat the daylight out of me. There were days I went home with a broken shoe or a ripped uniform or unraveled hair because I'd been in a fight.

I thought about telling my family, but I was afraid they would confront her parents and that would make her even more upset at me. I kept this up for weeks, being intimidated and dodging and quickly disappearing right after school until I was certain things were clear. The kids at my school were having fun watching Erica bully me almost every day. They looked forward to the event, and when I dodged the bullet, they would always ask the following day where I'd been after school the previous day.

It went on like this for a few weeks until just before the end of the school year; we were going to have our annual school concert. I had bought tickets to the concert and I was silently praying that Erica wasn't going to attend. The day of the concert came and I quickly asked my friend if she knew whether or not Erica would be attending. By midafternoon, she delivered the bad news: Erica would be there. My friend Andrea sadly looked at me and asked, "What are you going to do? Are you going to leave early to avoid her?"

In that moment I cried as if my mother had died. I wanted to see the concert. I wanted to stay for the entire program, not just a portion of it, and I wanted to be able to joke around with my friends after the concert. But how was I going to do that if Erica was there? For the first time, I felt sad, helpless, hopeless, and violated—and I was petrified.

That was the day, the defining moment; the time had come. I had had enough of Erica's pushing me around. I was still afraid of her; after all, she was a bully, and she bullied anyone that got in her way. However, in that moment, I realized I was more afraid of spending the next two years of grade school being bullied and beaten up by this girl. I was more afraid of being afraid of her. In that moment, what I wanted—to watch the concert like a normal student without worrying about what would happen after the concert was over—was more important than my fear of Erica.

After the concert, we were all on our ways to our respective homes. Just as I'd thought, as soon as we were out of sight of the school, Erica started calling me names and some of the other kids started laughing. I didn't think twice about my response, because I had hardly thought about anything else during the entire concert. I had decided that that was the last day I would allow her to bully and humiliate me.

Before she could say another word, I had knocked her to the ground and I was beating on her for everything she had done to me. A few minutes later, a parent passing by decided to intervene and pull me from her.

I went to that grade school for another two years, and not only did Erica not utter another negative word to me, she never bullied anyone else at school. We even became close friends a few years later.

At the time, I didn't quite realize that my fear of the long-term turmoil this girl might put me through for at least another couple of years empowered me to stand up for myself. This goes to show the power of using fear to your advantage. My fear empowered me to make a tough decision—be afraid of her for the next two years of grade school or stand up for myself and enjoy the next two years of grade school!

The choice can be quite clear when you look at what's in front of you and the situation you are presented with.

The Truth about Fear

Did you know fear of failure is the number one reason most people never achieve their dreams or reach a fraction of their potential? Our fear of life's many "little things" often causes us to self-sabotage. In doing so, we give up on ourselves before we even get started. Most people do not realize that fear can be used as an ally; it is a powerful motivator. If used strategically, it can empower us to reach great heights. It's that natural intuition or emotion that ignites a fight-or-flight response in each of us. It can be used to achieve success in more ways than we would have thought possible.

If we allow our fear to defeat us, it could leave us feeling empty, stuck, or resentful; it might even cause us to give up on friendships or relationships and could possibly destroy our future and our lives. I dated a guy in high school who broke up with me because I was moving to another country. To my astonishment, his explanation was, "I love you, but I'm afraid you'll find someone else when you relocate. I'm not willing to take that chance, so let's call it a day." He went on to say he would rather take his chances with someone he could see every day. You see, even though we had something good going on between us, his fear of me finding someone else and abandoning him caused him to end a relationship and friendship that could have possibly blossomed into something great. Instead of taking things one day at a time, embracing and enjoying the time we spent together, and making plans to fill the distance gap, he made a life-changing decision out of fear—his fear of something that might never have happened!

This is a perfect example of how most of us operate. We give up on many things—our dreams, our aspirations, relationships, love, a chance to make a difference, and a life of abundance—before we even get started simply because of our fear.

But if we use fear advantageously, we can achieve and enjoy a future and a life filled with love, laughter, balance, many accomplishments, and an abundance of wealth—a life filled with success.

Fear is almost always present. However, only a handful of individuals have discovered the secret of using it to our advantage to achieve long-term wealth and sustainable success. In this book, I will be share the secret of using your fear to win every time.

After colliding head-on with fear a number of times and learning my share of lessons from the University of Hard Knocks, I discovered that even though we will never really be free from fear, there is something truly useful about it. I came to realize it can be used to our advantage if we choose to look at it objectively. It is important to remember that there are no "top secrets" to any given success; it all lies in the little things we already know, but often overlook for a number of reasons. Sometimes the answer is too close to us for us to identify, or it requires some sort of change.

Change requires you to step out of what you are comfortable with. More often than not, most of us opt to remain the same—because it's easier, it seems safer, it seems more secure, and we're not required to learn something new or do anything different. This is a primary example of how fear affects our everyday lives and contributes to the decisions we make.

Because of our fear of failure we often choose not to try new things, and even when we take a step forward, because of our fear we are hesitant to follow through and see our vision to the end. Consequently, decisions like this will result in failure. Keep in mind that it's impossible for us to get ahead if while we are moving forward, we are always looking behind.

It makes you wonder doesn't it? You think you are saving yourself the angst of failure, but what you've done instead is to create the road map leading directly to failure when you make such decisions!

Call to Action

What are some of the things you fear?

My fears are

_____

_____

_____

_____

Chapter Two

Perceptions

If you think you can do a thing or think you can't do a thing, you're right.

—Henry Ford

Good or bad, it starts with the mind.

Just a few weeks back, my brother was struggling to let go of a failed business venture and I tried to give him some advice. During our conversation he asked me, "What do you know about failing? You've never failed in a day in your life." At first I was a bit taken aback. I was not expecting that question; even though I knew I must have failed at some point in my life, it took me a few minutes to compose myself and think hard to remember the times.

As I paused to think about it, I learned something very important about myself and my perception of things. It's not that I haven't failed; I've had my fair share of failures. I realized my perspective gave my failures an unusual spin. Instead of just viewing my missteps or speed bumps as failures, I saw them as part of my journey to my ultimate destination.

I've learned more from the mistakes I've made than from the successes I've had. Even though it's difficult at times, I try to make a conscious attempt to take the lessons and look for the opportunities in each situation. Most importantly, as I went through those difficult times, I didn't see myself "as is" during those moments; I saw myself as what I wanted to be once I overcame those obstacles.

Call to Action

Start by looking at things from a different point of view; your response to a particular situation and your perception of things will always contribute to the outcome.

If your perception is a negative one, you're almost guaranteed to have a negative outcome. Start seeing the glass as "half full" instead of "half empty" and your positive thoughts will attract the results you desire.

There is always a lesson from an experience and almost always an underlying opportunity. Because of our egos and our emotions (two big E's that results in failure), when we are faced with these types of experiences, we typically lose focus, but this is when we need to stay focused. We need to let go of the notion that we've made a mistake. So what if we made a mistake or failed at something? It's not the end of the world! What are we going to do differently the next time around?

In life, experience will always be your best teacher, so why would you want to give up such an invaluable learning opportunity simply because of fear?

Don't let the fear of failure deter you from taking your life to new heights. The successful minds of the world look at mistakes as **outcomes** or **results**, not as failures.

What would you like to achieve that you've been putting off for so long because of fear? What dream have you given up that you need to dust off and bring to life?

The reality is that you will fail at some point; it's inevitable. **It comes down to what scares you the most. Is it trying and failing *or* not making an attempt and having to live with mediocre results?**

Now what if you tried and failed? Not a big deal. Yes, you'll be disappointed. Yes, you may lose a night or two of sleep, maybe you'll cry a few tears. However, what you should be more afraid of is not trying and then being disappointed in the direction and outcome of your life. You should fear the resentment you'll have toward others and yourself for making a decision to live a mediocre life because of fear.

I can just about hear you saying to yourself, *Not me. I'd be paralyzed with humiliation—what would my family think? What would my friends think?* The reality is, the few friends and family members that truly matter would have an enormous amount of respect for you. They would recognize that you tried, and if they supported your vision yesterday, they'll still support your vision tomorrow.

On the other hand, the critics are and will remain exactly as they are and probably will always be—critics! They will always look for your shortcomings and use them against you in whatever way they can. Whether you succeeded or failed, they would still be critical and judgmental of your decisions. This is because of their own lack of confidence to even dream to do the things you are pursuing. Why do you need their approval to dream *your* dreams and fulfill *your* destiny? You may never get approval from them; never seek someone else's agreement in order to go after the things you desire or want. The higher up the food chain you go, the more critics you'll have.

Some of you may still be reluctant. If you are like me; this is because one of your biggest critics is probably you. You'll need to learn to silence that little voice that tells you that you can't or it's impossible. Why live your life fearing something that may never happen?

Why not enjoy what's in front of you by leveraging the opportunities that come along?

Let me stop here for a minute and ask you this. What if you succeed at your new venture? What an accomplishment it would be! Wouldn't it be worth it to find out?

Call to Action

Give yourself permission to do the things you want to do—to be who you want to become—and to pursue your passion and purpose, whatever it may be.

Identify and make a list of all the things you are giving yourself permission to do.

I, _____ give myself permission to
    (Your Name)

When I was a child, I discovered something unique about myself. I loved to write; I would sit and write for hours. Regardless of the emotion I was feeling—whether I was happy, sad, upset, hurt, or disappointed—I would grab a pencil and paper and put my thoughts in print. Writing was my partner; it listened to me when no one else did. It gave me my "inner joy." It often gave me the voice I was not always confident I had.

Do you have anything that you do that makes you feel like that? It may be singing, writing, giving speeches, teaching, or helping others. Write down the thing that you do that gives you your **"inner joy."**

_____

_____

Ironically at that time, I didn't have a story to tell. I just knew I loved to write something, anything—poetry, stories, letters, songs. I remember sitting on my grandmother's porch, anxiously waiting for the Sunday newspaper, so that I could read and critique the poems in the obituary column. As you can imagine, this is definitely not normal for the average eleven-year-old.

Seeing my interest, my family would encourage me. They often purchased other newspapers and magazines for me. Whenever I read the posts written in the papers, I would revise them, adding my own flare by rearranging or rewriting to make what I thought would be a better read.

I wasn't talented enough to recite my writings, nor could I sing a line of the songs I wrote, but something about expressing myself on paper empowered me. There was something in the things I wrote that kept my hope alive, and something about them seemed to inspire a certain type of people. I soon discovered my writings provided others with hope!

Even though I received mostly great reviews, I also heard negative remarks from naysayers. It was very discouraging to hear the responses when I told a few classmates that I wanted to enter our school's annual writing competition. Most of them advised me against entering; they would say things like, "People do not like poetry and love songs," or, "Motivational quotes are not bestsellers."

I struggled for days to get past those comments; they were painful to hear. In my mind, I began to struggle with the decision of whether or not to enter the competition. Although I was passionate about writing, I began to fear because of other people's opinions. I was terrified of being rejected and even more afraid of losing the competition.

Through all of this, I kept hearing one friend's voice in my head reminding me that he was inspired by the things I wrote and saying that the world could benefit from them as well. I had to decide what I was more fearful of. I decided to enter the writing competition, and the unexpected happened. I not only won the competition, but I also won the school district award for the most inspirational work.

You see, I entered that competition even though I was afraid of losing and having the naysayers remind me that they had told me so; I was more afraid to give up on my writing, the one thing at the time that defined me. I was afraid of not being able to express myself and my thoughts—not being able to make a difference in someone's life through the words I wrote. Had I listened to the negative remarks and given up there and then, I'd probably be wondering today what the outcome might have been had I at least tried.

Have you given up on doing something because of someone else's opinions?

_____

Do you sabotage the results before the race has even begun?

_____

How does it make you feel when you make such decisions?

_____

Be very wise when it comes to taking other people's opinions about yourself, your goals, or your aspirations. Most times, they have alternate motives for the opinions they express. It's important to surround yourself with people who are of the same mind-set as you, people who are heading in the same direction in terms of their aspirations and their ability to follow through on their objectives. Others who do not share the same perspective will almost always have a different spin on things. It's not that they are bad people; they are just not mentally and emotionally at the place you may be. Sometimes you'll need to become emotionally strong enough before you share certain things with some of the people surrounding you.

Fear in any shape or form is never easy to control. However, it can be leveraged and used to your advantage if you choose to look at it objectively. You have to be able to see your goal, believe it, and want it badly. What will your choice be?

I will be showing you how to leverage your fear, so that you too can achieve success in any area of your life. Keep reading to find out how you also can accomplish this successfully.

Chapter Three

The Two Types of Fear

Failure is simply the opportunity to begin again,
this time more intelligently.

—Henry Ford

In order to use fear to our advantage, it's important to understand the emotion itself. We need to realize that it's not necessarily fear that affects us, but our perception of it. Whether the fear we are feeling is a "healthy fear" or not, we tend to perceive it to be more than it is in all cases.

We must acknowledge that fear is a natural part of our lives and we'll never really be rid of fear; there is always something to fear. The closest we'll come to overcoming it is if we use it to our advantage by leveraging it. This is done by choosing to fear the right things or the things I will refer to as the essentials.

FEAR is defined as being afraid or feeling anxious or apprehensive about a possible or probable situation or event.

FEAR can be broken down into two types. I've defined each type; following are viable examples of each.

1. **Fear of the Essentials.** Some examples are the following: fear of a life of mediocrity, fear of not achieving a fraction of your potential

2. **Fear of the Non-essentials.** Some examples are the following: fear of failure, fear of success, fear of rejection, fear of change

The **Essentials** are defined as the things that are absolutely necessary. The **Non-essentials** are defined as the things having little or no importance, not necessary. (My definitions are taken from Princeton University's WordNet, a "lexical database for English.")

It's obvious which of these makes more long-term sense—the essentials. Anything that is absolutely necessary is worth fearing. These are the things that will have the greatest impact on your life. If you do not have or achieve an essential, it could potentially be detrimental to you, your well-being, your future, your life, or your success.

It's extremely easy to confuse the two; consequently, most people become paralyzed by fear and adapt the philosophy that the fear of anything and **everything** is essential. They often neglect to distinguish between the two types of fear, which is similar to the distinction between a need and a want.

TRAINING YOUR MIND TO USE FEAR AS AN EMPOWERMENT TOOL

Everyone struggles with fear at one point or another, and the vast majority will not achieve any level of success or reach a fraction of their potential in their lifetime simply because of their fear. Only a few very successful people have trained their minds to use fear as an empowerment tool. Think about it. Fear is manifested in the mind, right? Who controls your mind? Of course *you* do! However, as simple as this is, we often forget.

Fear is able to manifest itself in our minds. The key is to use our minds to manipulate it, by being selective and choosing to have a healthy fear of the essential things. If we learn to use this selectivity as our advantage tool, we'll be on our way to success.

Don't waste time being fearful of the non-essentials, or the "little things." These don't contribute much. They have the least amount of impact on your life, and most importantly, they can be eliminated or reduced by creating a plan, by doing your due-diligence, by conducting research, by having a coach or mentor, or by doing many other things.

What Makes Us Different

Average Minds

Average individuals spend time fearing the small **non-essentials** of life, like what people would say if they failed; the lifestyle changes they would be faced with if they failed, or the humiliation it would cause. Average minds are more concerned about protecting their egos, which ironically will keep them stuck where they are and forever average, thus ensuring failure. They spend most of their time telling you why something can't and won't work.

Extraordinary Minds

Extraordinary individuals are high achievers who realize a life of wealth and success. They choose to fear the **essentials**, the way life would be if they didn't go after their dreams, what their legacy would be if they chose to fear the "little things" and remain stuck where they are today. They view failure as not making an attempt to do something, not trying to solve a problem, not aspiring and working toward creating something and developing the next big thing. They spend their time making things happen.

It is crucial to understand and decide whether you want to be or remain average or become extraordinary. Don't be discouraged if you currently fall into the "average minds" category, as long as you make the choice not to remain there. Most of us start in that category, and the rest of us have been there at one point or another.

I once had a neighbor who saw the need for an apartment building in our community. There were a lot of things happening in our community, like new infrastructure and an expansion of the school district. Therefore, there would be new teachers moving into the community and they would be looking for somewhere to call home. There was great demand for rental properties. My neighbor had the vision, but he only had enough money to purchase the land, and not to develop the land or build the apartment building. In spite his lack of capital to complete the project, he decided he would purchase the land and worry about the funding sometime in the near future.

A few months after he purchased the land, an out-of-town developer approached him about the project; this developer didn't have the vision, but he saw the opportunity. He agreed to finance the project for my neighbor, and they agreed this developer would get a percentage of the profit once the project was complete.

My neighbor recalls, "Yes, I was very afraid. I knew I didn't have enough money to execute my vision, and what was worse was, I had no idea if or where I would get the funds to fund this project. However, when it came down to it, I was more afraid of losing sight of my vision and missing out on a great opportunity, so I decided it was worth the risk. If I hadn't been able to develop it, I still would have been able to make a profit a few years down the road just from acquiring the land, so I really didn't have anything to lose, and I had everything to gain."

How many of us would have passed up on our vision and this opportunity because of our fear of a non-essential?

Call to Action

Use your fear of the essentials as a motivator to harness and prepare yourself for your ultimate objective every time you are hesitant to follow through on your:

- Visions

- Projects

- Business/Personal objectives

- Dreams

- Great friendship or relationship

- Passion

- Aspirations

- Financial objectives

Think of the emotion you are feeling and ask yourself this simple question:

Is my fear an "essential" or a "non-essential" one?

If it's a non-essential one, reduce or eliminate it by preparing yourself through your due-diligence process; this is sure to reduce or even eliminate your concerns.

If it's an essential fear, one that leaves that feeling in the pit of your stomach when you think of what you'll lose if you don't at try, that's when you **leverage** your essential fear by **allowing** it to motivate you to make a decision or to do what's in front of you!

Chapter Four

Fear can SAVE you from yourself!

One of the greatest discoveries a man makes, one of his great surprises, is to find he can do what he was afraid he couldn't do.

—Henry Ford

Using fear as a motivator and to your advantage

Not too long before I made the decision to officially retire from my nine to five job, I found myself in a situation that most of you probably have been in or are currently in. Let me emphasize that I've always had the mind of an entrepreneur. I was always coming up with business ideas, seeking out business opportunities, helping people with business concepts, and willing to solve a problem and make some money during the process.

At nine years old, in grade school, I was the in-class convenience store. I sold an assortment of candies and snacks; I saw a problem and made a business to solve it. I started putting my lunch money aside, and after a few weeks, I had saved up enough to purchase one small bag of candy. I later borrowed money from my mother, grandmother, and uncles to purchase more varieties, like gumballs and marbles. As you can see, I was leveraging other people's money from an early age.

I started selling my supplies to my classmates. When I'd sold the first bag, I had made back my original investment, plus enough to purchase two extra bags of candies. At one point, my "mobile candy business" was booming and it began drawing so much attention, I was almost suspended from school. I was told by my teacher, "You are here to get an education, not to operate a business." Imagine that! Her opinion did not stop me, as I quickly realized the power of being an entrepreneur.

I would joyfully tell anyone who would listen all the things I was going to do when I grew up. I was going to become a powerful and successful businesswoman. I would own many businesses employing thousands of people, and I would become very famous and wealthy.

As you may imagine, I was full of life and short on everything but dreams.

Given my early business venture, I'm certain you are not surprised that one of my greatest aspirations was to become a full-time entrepreneur, building successful businesses—working for myself, doing what I want, when I want.

I'm considered an expert in several fields. I am extremely talented when it comes to being innovative and strategic, and I have founded several lucrative and successful businesses. I've worked as an expert in the legal and financial industries and consulted for entrepreneurs and coached/mentored many aspiring entrepreneurs to success. But it still took me over ten years to make the decision to transition into my passion and purpose, so don't be discouraged if this is where you are today.

I had just made a goal to work for another year and then retire from being an employee so as to build my business and become an Author, Real Estate Entrepreneur, and Strategist-Mentor for Entrepreneurs.

At the time, I was working for a top financial company in a leadership role, working my tail off holding the department together. I was working a four-person job by myself and getting and maintaining the numbers. I was approached by the company's human resources department to interview for a more senior leadership position in another department. In this new role, I would be making a great six figure income. I was hesitant at first because I knew I had a bigger and better long-term plan that was more suited to me.

Nonetheless, the more I thought about it, the better the opportunity sounded, and I grew excited over time. My original plan slowly started to be placed on the back burner, as I began to think how much further this new role could take me in my career. Even though my career focus had always been to become an entrepreneur, doing what I loved, I thought of and convinced myself of all the ways this job could work for me and how good it would look to the people in my life. Of course, this went against everything I had planned, wanted, and envisioned for myself, but in my mind, it was an attractive opportunity.

I thought to myself, financially I would be able to put some more money aside, make a few more real estate purchases, expand my real estate business, and gain a bit more job security. Since we were in the midst of an economic recession, maybe it would be a good thing to hold on to the job until things started to turn around in the economy.

I convinced myself this senior leadership role would look great on my résumé once I made the decision to resign. What résumé? What was I thinking? Why would I even care about having a good résumé? I had no intention of remaining an employee much longer, right?

I had totally lost focus of who I was, where I wanted to go, and my objectives. In my mind, I was trading in a long-term sustainable profit, financial independence, financial freedom, and my time to work for a paycheck, and maybe, just maybe, if I was lucky, I might get a small pension when I reached the age of sixty-five.

I completed the three interviews and passed the assessment test with flying colors. They checked my references and things were looking great. **Until** . . .

Sudden disaster hit. A senior manager in my department called the hiring department and said I was too critical to the immediate team and that they were not willing to authorize the transfer. That's all it took to go up into flames. Fortunately for me, I had my "aha" moment and my reality check.

As you may imagine, I was devastated. I hadn't anticipated the results, at least not this one. My fear of reliving that situation quickly snapped me back into reality; that **FEAR** changed my perspective on the outcome. Thank goodness, the outcome reminded me of my original plan and objectives.

I reiterated to myself why being an entrepreneur was always at the forefront of my mind, why I had figured out the importance of being an entrepreneur at age nine. Most companies have no loyalty to employees. As an employee, you have very limited control over your career prospects, over your dreams, over what you are called to do, and over how far you'll go in an organization. We sometimes live under the illusion that we have job stability and security, which is not the case in most organizations.

I made a promise to myself then never to allow anyone or any organization—with the exception of the ones I owned—to determine how far I'd go and when I'd get there. I had one of the most important lessons of my life from that experience; it was a priceless one that you, too can learn from.

Ultimately, my fear of a few ESSENTIALS saved me from myself. Here are some of the essentials I feared in that situation:

- **My fear of reliving the situation I found myself in**

- **My fear of living a life of mediocrity**

- **My fear of giving control of my future over to one person or organization that could make such a crucial decision affecting my life at any point**

- **My fear of being "stuck" where I was permanently**

- **My fear of not living my life with purpose or realizing my true potential**

- **My fear of settling and being disappointed in the outcome of my career**

- **My fear of always taking instructions from my boss**

- **My fear of never becoming or achieving more**

- **My fear of always punching someone else's clock**

These essential emotions quickly put things back into perspective.

Call to Action

Think about a similar situation you may be in (professional or personal) and make a list of your essential fears. Use them as your road map to guide you back to reality:

_____'s Current Essential Fears
(Your Name)

_____

_____

_____

_____

_____

_____

_____

_____

_____

_____

_____

_____

_____

_____

_____

While I was also fearful of a few non-essentials, the essentials were more critical, more relevant and absolutely necessary, than my fear of the non-essential emotions below.

My non-essential fears in this situation:

- Starting a new business

- Not having the security of a job

- Not having a steady pay-check

- Not being able to even predict whether or not my business of choice would succeed or fail

- Not knowing whether or not I'd get any clients to use my services or purchase my products

I was more fearful of the things listed on my essentials list than the things on my non-essential list.

Call to Action

Make a list of the non-essentials that you may be concerned about, relating to the same situation you've identified on your essentials list.

_____**'s Current Non-essential Fears**

(Your Name)

_____

_____

_____

_____

_____

_____

_____

_____

_____

_____

I proceeded to do research, make plans, and prepare to eliminate my fear of the non-essentials. Here are some of the things I did:

- I did extensive research on the market I was getting into and the niche I was targeting. This reduced my concern about the market and whether or not it would fail.

- Since there would be no steady paycheck (at least temporarily), I created a financial plan, which included setting money aside and constructing multiple streams of income to ensure I would be able to take care of my financial obligations. I started writing, offering consulting services, etc.

- I created and executed a strong marketing plan to counteract the concern about whether or not I'd get clients. Nothing beats a good marketing plan!

Call to Action

Draft a plan that applies to your individual scenario for how you can reduce or eliminate each one of the things you've identified on your non-essentials list.

A little secret:

1. Keep it as simple as you can.

2. Work on each one, one at a time.

_____'s **Proactive Plan**

(Your Name)

_____

_____

_____

_____

_____

_____

_____

_____

_____

_____

_____

_____

_____

_____

_____

_____

_____

_____

_____

_____

_____

_____

_____

_____

_____

_____

_____

Through this experience, even though I was afraid. I did not allow myself to be paralyzed by fear; I was able to capitalize on or leverage my fear of the essentials. I allowed them to motivate and empower me, thus creating and sustaining an enormous level of success.

My **FEAR** of the essentials drove me right into:

- My commitment to doing what I love

- Finding what I'm passionate about

- Finding my true purpose

- Seeking financial freedom

- Creating long-term sustainable wealth

- Building Success

- Controlling my own destiny

- Spending more time with my loved ones and recognizing what's important

- Doing what I want, when I want, how I want

- Helping others to achieve the same level of success

Wouldn't you like to achieve an abundance of these things and more for yourself and your family and help others to do the same?

Below is a list of possible essential items to get you started. I've broken them down into two main sub-groups for you. Remember to fear the ESSENTIALS and win every time!

Possible ESSENTIALS to be fearful of:

Professional Essential Fears

- Fear of taking instructions from your boss for the rest of your career

- Fear of not becoming your own boss

- Fear of wondering to yourself in thirty years what would have happened if you had tried, if you had pursued your dreams

- Fear of living paycheck to paycheck for the rest of your life

- Fear of not having the career you want, because you didn't believe in yourself and your capabilities

- Fear of giving up too soon

- Fear of settling for less than you deserve

Personal and General Essential Fears

- Fear of not becoming financial independent

- Fear of the future you will have if you have no plan in place

- Fear of the legacy you'll pass on to your children and grandchildren

- Fear of your children living the life you've lived and or worked hard to stay away from

- Fear of the outcome if you don't teach your children about their relationship to money

- Fear of not reaching your true potential and fulfilling your purpose

- Fear of what your life will look like when you reach the age of retirement

- Fear of reaching the age of retirement and realizing you don't have enough money to live comfortably for the remainder of your life

- Fear of reaching the age of sixty-five and having to get a job at local store in order to purchase the bare essentials, like food and medication

- Fear of being stuck where you are as you are forever

- Fear of living a life of mediocrity, not reaching for your best

- Fear of living an unhappy life

- Fear of living an unhealthy life

- Fear of losing a friend over insecurities

- Fear of not giving yourself a chance to be loved

- Fear of the outcome of living in an unhealthy relationship for the rest of your life

- Fear of living the life you've lived in the past, repeating it

- Fear of letting someone else's opinion define what you do and what you can achieve

- Fear of living an unfulfilled life full of "what ifs," "I should haves" and "if I had known" later on

- Fear of not forgiving yourself for past mistakes

- Fear of not forgiving others so that you can step into your life of abundance

Call to Action

Expand on this by creating and adding your own list of essentials, the things worth fearing. You can have as many sub-groups as you'd like.

Remember, the essentials are things that are absolutely necessary. If you forget at any time, go back to chapter three and revisit the definitions of both types of fear. This will allow you to identify the type you are faced with.

_____'s **Professional Essential Fears**

(Your Name)

_____

_____

_____

_____

_____

_____

_____

_____

_____

_____

_____'s Personal and General Essential Fears

(Your Name)

_____

_____

_____

_____

_____

_____

_____

_____

_____

_____

_____

_____

_____

_____

_____

_____

_____

_____

_____

_____

_____

_____

_____

_____

We get side-tracked at one point or another; therefore, I can't stress enough how extremely important it is to journal your objectives, where you are currently and where you want to go; the steps you are going to take, and *why* you want to achieve them. This will provide you with clarity; it will also remind and assist you to stay focused and on track.

Obstacles will arise and sometimes you'll need to take a detour onto another route, or find ways to go around an obstacle; the destination remains the same, so be flexible, as this, too, is part of the process.

Don't become frustrated because you have to make a few changes along the way. This is what makes the journey interesting, and most importantly, this is where you'll see and be able to seize new opportunities. Don't allow yourself to become discouraged because the plan may have changed. Remember, it's not only about the plan; it's about where you are today and your destination, and there are many ways to get there.

I am not here to tell you that fear does not exist, because it does; I won't tell you it's easy to control, but you can choose to fear the right things. With that choice, fear can become a life-changing experience.

With the right mind-set and your flexibility to be objective, you can make the right choices and achieve anything.

As a child growing up in the beautiful and sunny Caribbean island of Jamaica, life was not always easy for me. I was the eldest of three children and was raised by my mother, a single mom who worked extremely hard to make ends meet. She would often work two or three jobs just so that we could afford the necessities that most kids take for granted today.

Life definitely had its twists and turns and was not a bed of roses for us, but nonetheless I was happy, ambitious, smart, confident, and always hopeful that one day I would have the life I wanted and would be able to provide my mother with the life she deserved to have, the one she worked hard to achieve but could never afford all those years ago.

Seeing my mother struggle the way she did when I was a child changed my life, built my character, and gave me the tenacity to go after so much more.

Growing up, just the thought of living the life my mother lived scared me into creating my own path whenever one didn't exist and exploring avenues I probably wouldn't have explored.

This **fear** has enabled me to develop a new perspective on life, business, and things in general. I choose not to entertain or allow myself to see anything other than the results I wanted. I always view the glass half full instead of half empty.

Even though I was also afraid of other things, nothing was more compelling and motivating than my **fear** of living the life I've lived through my mother's experiences. Of course, at that time, I couldn't articulate that it was my fear that started my attraction to certain things that would ultimately allow me to live the life of my dreams. As I became older, I realized, without fully understanding, that I had learned and mastered the power of **fear** and how to use it successfully to my advantage. I was fearful of the right things, the things that would have the most impact on my life—the essential things!

Call to Action

What are some of the essentials that you are afraid of that will have the most impact on your life? Once you've identified your essentials, commit yourself fully and allow them to empower and motivate you, by investigating how you are going to achieve your objectives or how you are going to prevent the unforeseen from happening.

*It's okay if some of the things on this list are also on one of the other Call to Action lists discussed in the earlier chapters.

_____'s Essential Fears that can have the most impact on my life

(Your Name)

_____

_____

_____

_____

_____

_____

_____

_____

Shanna McFarlane

_____

_____

_____

_____

_____

_____

_____

_____

_____

Chapter Five

HARNESS your FEAR of

the Non-essentials

The fear of not achieving our ultimate objectives
should always outweigh the fear of trying and failing,
if we are open and honest with ourselves
—Shanna McFarlane

I know some of you have spent most of your lives fearing the non-essentials, or the "little things." Therefore it's not easy for you to shift your focus to the essentials. Your opinion of fear is that it's always an essential. To assist those of you who feel this way, I've listed some steps you can take to reduce or eliminate your fear of the non-essentials. These steps will enable you to focus on fearing the essentials.

Call to Action

1. **Acknowledge your fear, but don't be paralyzed by it.** There is a huge difference between acknowledging and being paralyzed.

   ♣ Write down your concerns, and across from them, write **how** or **what** you could do to eliminate those concerns, or at the very least reduce them

   ♣ Follow through by taking **action** on your responses above (the hows and whats) in reducing or eliminating those concerns

2. **Prepare yourself.** Answer the questions that are causing you to fear the non-essentials. Do this by:

   ♣ Educating yourself on the things you are unfamiliar with

   ♣ Asking yourself how and what you'll need in order to achieve your objectives

These will answer a lot of the questions that are causing you to be paralyzed by a non-essential fear.

3. **Get clarity.** A combination of one and two will provide you with the basic tools for achieving clarity. Ask yourself questions such as:

- ♣ Why do I feel afraid?

- ♣ What am I afraid of?

- ♣ How can I stop this from happening?

- ♣ What's the **essential** that I really should be concerned about?

- ♣ What's the worst that can happen if I make an attempt to achieve something and I fail? (You'll be surprised the answer is not nearly as bad as not making an attempt.)

- ♣ Are there any reasons I'm not identifying? This will allow you to search deeper for answers that will allow you to be more comfortable in order to move to the next level.

_____'s **Steps for eliminating my fear of the non-essentials.**

(Your Name)

_____

_____

_____

_____

_____

_____

_____

_____

_____

_____

A Practical example of an "Essential" fear and leveraging it to your advantage

Fearing an Essential

Scenario 1

You fear reaching the age of retirement and realize you're entitled to less pension than you thought you would be getting. To top it off, you still have a mortgage payment and not enough income to support your debt and your everyday essentials (medications, etc.). Based on this you would be forced to go out and get a job at your local store, working full-time and making minimum wage. Yikes!

Thinking about this. How does it make you feel?

Petrified, probably. Right?

Using this FEAR as a MOTIVATOR

This fear can empower you to create a financial plan for your future starting now.

(1) Save. You can ensure this wouldn't happen to you by starting to put money away today. Save a portion of what you earn, whether it's through putting a certain amount into a bank account once or twice per month, or investing in a retirement or education fund. It does accumulate over time!

Another way you can do this, and my personal favorite, is to create leveraged income or multiple streams of income (some of you know this as passive income) by building assets that will provide you with long-term sustainable cash flow over and over. A few examples to achieve this are:

(2) Become a strategic entrepreneur. Strategic entrepreneurs not only look for opportunities, they look for ways to solve problems. They acknowledge it's impossible to be good at everything and they have no intentions of even attempting, as that's a recipe for frustration and disastrous results; however they are strategic enough to use their strength, doing what they are good at and leveraging the rest by using the services of others. A few simple things you could do are:

Sell your ideas. Sounds simple, doesn't it? If you are someone with an innovative mind that is filled with an abundance of great ideas, but you have no intention of becoming an entrepreneur, why give them away for free? You could make easy income by selling them. You can do this by working as a consultant or a coach.

Buy someone else's ideas. If, unlike the scenario above, you're short on ideas, you may not have the idea, but you could sure create a successful business from one. Seek out consultants in this field. Choose your idea or your niche and focus on solving a problem around that niche; there are tons of problems to be solved; you'd be surprised!

(3) Start a business. It can be home based and/or online. A good way to come up with an idea for this category is to answer the questions, "What problem would I be solving? What challenges am I faced with in my everyday life? What do people tell me they wish they had?"

Many times, some of the best business ideas are staring us right in the face, but we are waiting for someone else to solve the problem.

Get rid of the notion that you have to know or like a particular industry to create a successful business from it; the reality is, you don't. "Liking" a certain industry is not one of the fundamentals in building a successful and profitable business.

As a matter of fact, if you base your business idea solely on what you like, regardless of whether there is a problem that you'll be solving, you will be making an emotional decision. In business, emotion is one of the surest and fastest paths to failure.

You can offer your services by performing them yourself, by working from home or part-time, but my personal recommendation is to always hire and train people to see your vision. If you employ them to do the work, you collect a portion of the income for doing almost nothing. There is nothing wrong in doing this; you are creating viable employment for people who are willing to work and get paid for doing so.

This is called leveraging the service of employees, and all parties involved get to reap the benefits!

(4) **Invest in real estate as a business**. This is one of my favorite strategies. Use a defined strategy to build equity and generate cash flow while you increase your portfolio. If you purchase rental properties and use a defined strategy, you could benefit in more ways than one by leveraging the bank's money, leveraging the time invested by using a property manager, and having your tenants pay down your mortgage.

(5) **Write a book**. Put all the knowledge, expertise, and experiences you've had over the years into a book or an e-book. It could be:

-A memoir
-An information product
-A self-help product

Create this type of product once and it will generate income for a long time.

Additional Examples of "Essential" Fears—Leveraging Them to Your Advantage

Fearing the Essentials

Scenario 2

Fear of settling and living a life of mediocrity

Using this FEAR as a MOTIVATOR

This fear can empower you to create a life filed with abundance, you achieve this by:

(1) Stepping out of your comfort zone to explore ways to have a life of abundance

(2) Think about the different ways that you can achieve the life you want and apply it!

Scenario 3

Fear of not fulfilling your purpose

Using this FEAR as a MOTIVATOR

This fear can empower you to search or explore deep within yourself to find out what your true purpose is. What are you good at? What truly makes you happy? What do you love to do? How can you genuinely serve the people around you?

You can find out what your purpose is by asking yourself what you do that has the most impact on people. Some are good at motivating others through talking, some through writing. For some, it may be their compassion and genuine caring for people. Others may be gifted entertainers (comedy, film, sports). Explore and find out what's yours!

Scenario 4

Fear of missing out on a chance to love and to be loved

Using this FEAR as a MOTIVATOR

This fear can empower you to let go and go with the flow. Giving love and being loved is a great thing. You don't want to waste an entire lifetime, missing out on happiness simply because of a bad past experience. You would be punishing yourself for someone else's mistake or loss.

You deserve all the great things life has to offer, and love is one of them. Ask yourself what is the worst that can happen. Is it that it may not work out? How do you expect to meet the right person without giving it a try? (What if it does work out?)

Scenario 5

Fear of not advancing in your career because of limited advanced education

Using this FEAR as a MOTIVATOR

This fear can empower you to refocus on your objectives and it can also force you to make a commitment to do things that will advance you in your career. It looks a lot more achievable if you break it down to step-by-step pieces:

(1) Make a plan and stick to it as much as possible

(2) Go back to school. Maybe it has to be part time due to finances or family obligations, but you can take one course at a time instead of being overwhelmed with several, or you can take courses online.

(3) Think about the career you are in and where you would like to get in that field, and then investigate the qualifications you need in order to get there. Then take the required learning and development programs that will qualify you to get there!

I've heard many, many people say, "If I had my life to live over again, I would do this or that differently." Most people spend years saying this line over and over, making me wonder if they really had a chance to do it over, would they do anything differently? Or would they continue their lives fearing the non-essentials instead of the essential things?

Instead of spending time acknowledging the things you would do differently, use the fear of living a life you don't want motivate you into action today!

There you have it. You've just leveraged a few essential fears and used them to empower you to make plans and take action to protect your future. It's that simple.

Think about this for a minute or two. Sometimes it takes a little bit of time and focus to digest this information, especially since fear is standing right next to you, telling you you'll fail.

Read this information more than once and complete the Call to Action steps. I can't stress how important it is to complete this.

You will get a lot of vital information just by reading this book, however, in order for it to have the most impact on your life and your particular situation, you must complete the Call to Action steps. Some people might not get it and some probably never will, because they are not at that place where they are willing to make the choice or take the chance at doing something different.

Attitude is a choice, and it's everything when it comes to learning something new; most people fail to see that their attitudes contribute to the outcome of their lives.

Again, it comes back to fear of a **non-essential**. These people fear change, fear the outcome before it even happens and don't like not knowing what to expect. I know you are not one of those individuals, because you've taken the important first step of seeking the knowledge and expertise of others to assist you in moving beyond your fear. This alone sets you apart from the masses and positions you on your way to success.

Remember, you are not alone on this journey. Many have done it successfully, including me. Therefore, even though you may be afraid of taking that first step, the experiences outlined in this book are coming straight from the heart from someone who has walked in your shoes and wants to share with you the power of using fear. You are no different from me or anyone else that has done this. You, too, can leverage your fear and achieve the level of success you desire and truly deserve!

Spend some time clearing your head of the non-essential fears, or at the very least, work at reducing them. They take up most of your time and energy, and they are the ones that can be fixed the most easily.

Clear your mind of your previous perception of fear in order to solidify your mind-set regarding this new information. Read, meditate on the things outlined in this book, and then follow them closely. It has been proven; it works. It will take some work for you to step out of your comfort zone and rethink your focus.

If you are being paralyzed by fear and would like to remove the limitations it has made for you, give it a chance. Give yourself permission to move into the next phase of your life. You deserve all that the universe has in store for you. Don't become or remain an "average mind." Start living today. This is only the beginning!

Chapter Six

Going Forward

There is no greater agony than bearing an untold story inside you

—Maya Angelou

Going forward, the key questions are these:

If you were to allow your fear to deter you from trying to achieve your objective, whether it be achieving financial independence, creating a successful business, mastering something new, or embracing a new friendship or relationship . . .

Would you be comfortable with the results, knowing that it's possible you could do so much more, knowing with a little effort you could reach a new mountain and get a better view of the world and all that it has to offer?

If you allow your fear of the non-essentials to stop you, will you be satisfied living in the situation you are currently living in or the circumstance you are creating and heading toward?

The reality is that every successful person has had to step outside of his or her comfort zone. They had to give up who they were and reinvent themselves in order to achieve their objectives. They were all empowered at one point by FEAR; let the fear of remaining the same catapult you into doing new and better things.

Building something new can be uncomfortable, and being uncomfortable is ultimately the key that will challenge you to achieve things you would never have guessed you had in you.

These are all proven strategies that I personally have used to transform my ideas and visions into successful businesses, as have some of the most successful men and women around the globe. In doing so, we have given up a life of the mediocre and ordinary to create a life of abundance and the extraordinary.

Fear has been a driving factor in every success I have achieved. I have been able to use it to my advantage in one way or another; it is because of fear that I have been able to create the path to my own success, not leaving it to chance or putting my future in the hands of someone else. Because of this, I have been able to create the life I want on my own terms.

Most people spend a lifetime trying to get away from fear or trying to control it using the wrong approach. I have given you the foundation. The rest is straightforward, simple, and totally up to you!

Call to Action:

What are the dreams that you are holding back?

_____

_____

What are the aspirations you've laid to rest?

_____

_____

What business ideas have you been sitting on?

_____

_____

Where is the entrepreneurial spirit you once had?

_____

_____

Where is the creative side you have neglected to share with the world?

_____

_____

What talents have you hidden from the world?

_____

_____

What inspirational stories are you not sharing?

_____

_____

What career objective have you given up?

_____

_____

What are your life-long aspirations?

_____

_____

What do you want to achieve?

_____

_____

Where will you go from here?

_____

_____

What will you do tomorrow?

_____

_____

Whenever you fear something, go back to the fundamentals above and identify which category the fear you are feeling belongs to and ask yourself this question:

Is your fear an essential or a non-essential one? This answer will guide you on your way!

Chapter Seven

The power in using FEAR

Every accomplishment begins in your thoughts,
start by thinking BIG today.

—*Shanna McFarlane*

A life forever changed because of FEAR

Not too long ago, there was a young lady who found herself living on her own at the early age of sixteen; prior to this, she was full of life, ambitious, and confident. She had big dreams, but life had thrown her a few curve balls she was not prepared to deal with and she'd ended up living on her own. She had been through a difficult period of time and had spent the past six months going through some rough spots with family challenges. She had gone from being a straight-A student with a bright future to a future that didn't look so promising. She often wondered how and when she had gotten to that point.

In her heart, she started to view the world through a different set of eyes. Family members were cruel and she felt the people that should have taken care of her had done her a disservice by abandoning her. She spent at least five months being disappointed, angry, sad, bitter, embarrassed, and unforgiving of the things that had gone wrong in her life—until a stranger took the time to tell her, **"Never let someone else's opinion of you or your current situation determine who you are as a person or where and how far you can go."** This was her wake up call. These words transformed her perception of her situation and shed new light on the vision she once had for herself.

She started to make a life for herself, holding her head high, as she completed her studies and worked part-time to support herself. Things were going okay. She had just finished the last lap of high school and started completing her post-secondary studies. She was making ends meet and making every dollar count. She shared expenses with her roommate, and they conserved on everything from toilet paper to food supplies. Life was going okay.

Just over a year later, the unfortunate happened. The transit union in her community went on strike. With no means of transportation, she was forced to give up her job at a local supermarket, her only means of financial support. Within weeks, things started falling apart financially. Her landlord needed the rent, and with no job, the savings quickly ran out and this young woman ended up being evicted from her apartment.

As a last resort, she sought help at a local community shelter, hoping they would be able to assist her through her financial distress. Just over a week later, she chose not to comply with their requirements to accept social assistance due to her parents' sponsorship obligation, which would make them unable to help her siblings. Because of her decision she was given an ultimatum: take the assistance under the terms they were providing or leave. At first, she thought it was some sort of joke; she could not believe the system that was there to provide help would force her to make such a decision. She quickly discovered they were very serious, and when she stuck by her decision, she was also evicted from the shelter.

That was rock bottom for her. Things were out of control and pretty bad! With no family around, no money, and no one to help, she was forced to resort to begging outside the entrance to a grocery store. At the time, if her begging made her a dollar, she could buy a loaf of bread and margarine. That was her meal for an entire week.

She recalls that during those moments, most times she didn't have the strength or energy to cry. She was ambitious, and she had dreams and big plans for a bright future, but everything seemed to be working against her.

In order to get through each day, she had to change her perception of things. She made a conscious effort not to look at how she was living, not to wallow in self-pity, not to confine herself with the mentally of being a victim, and not to make any assumptions about herself as she was at that time. She kept remembering the words of that stranger she had met years before; this allowed her to believe there had to be more.

In the weeks to come, the city's transportation went back to normal, and with the help of a friend, she found a temporary place to call home. She landed another job and quickly enrolled in school to pursue her studies. She chose to have faith and to see herself as the person she wanted to be and knew she could become. With this focus, she fought her way and built a life filled with many accomplishments and successes.

A few years later, she decided to research what all billionaires and major corporations had in common. She had a goal to retire at an early age and she was curious and smart enough to know that if she wanted to achieve certain objectives, she should study the lives of the people who had done it successfully. She quickly discovered that what they all had in common was real estate; hence she decided to explore and build her own real estate investing business.

Today, she is a top business woman who is leaving her mark on everyone. She owns an empire in the business of real estate investing; she created a multi-million dollar real estate portfolio in less than eighteen months of investing in real estate, and she is the founder and

CEO of several successful businesses, she also educates and mentors on success and entrepreneurship.

She advises, "Fear has played a major role and is a top contributor to my success. There was never a dull or easy moment when you are fighting to stay true to yourself and your dreams." Her FEAR of reliving those circumstances, her FEAR of being homeless again, her FEAR of being in such a vulnerable situation where she would be forced to beg strangers' money so that she could have a meal, her FEAR of the humiliation she suffered in the process and her FEAR of not being strong enough to endure motivated and empowered her to believe in herself, to believe in and fight for her dreams, to be persistent, and to persevere regardless of the situation. These enabled her to build the life of wealth and success she enjoys today!

She wrote **this book to provide you with hope and to let you know that you, too, can use FEAR to your advantage simply by following the steps identified here.**

I am the young woman you just read about. This is my story and that was my life not too long ago!

Sometimes life is preparing us for what we could never dream of, and sometimes life is allowing us to live the story that will not only change our lives, but will contribute immensely to the lives of many generations to come. So don't be crippled by fear. It can do a lot more for you than just keep you down. You'll never see around the corner until you take the first step.

Remember that dream I had about becoming an author and a successful businesswoman? I had more than enough reasons to stop. Because of my fear of many different things, I could have chosen to be a victim, to remain where I was, to surrender to other people's opinions, to just accept what life presented to me, to quit before I started, to accept mediocrity, and to give up on my dreams. But I chose not to let all those things get in the way of what I wanted.

As difficult as it was, I kept going forward hoping for better but sometimes getting worse. Eventually, though, I got much better and much more than I could have hoped for!

Don't let FEAR stop you short of achieving your dreams. Embrace it like I did and have it change and improve your life forever.

Remember, fear exists whether we care to admit it or not. Its existence is beyond our control, so we must live with it. If you must live with it, why not have it work FOR YOU instead of against you?

*   *   *

**Don't forget to grab your FREE Bonuses
Shanna's Top Success Fundamentals for New and
Aspiring Entrepreneurs
Shanna's 6 Steps to Success Blueprint
Please send e-mail to: info@ShannaMcFarlane.com**

Shanna McFarlane International Corp. Resources

http://www.LeverageFearAndAchieveSuccess.com

http://www.ShannaMcFarlane.com

http://ShannaMcFarlaneCoachingForSuccess.com

Prepare to Win Audio Tele-Series

Talk-Success with Shanna

Leverage Fear and Achieve Success Audio Series

Success-In-A-Box Audio/Video Series with Editions on:
—Strategic Entrepreneurship-The Business Woman in You edition
—Strategic Youth Entrepreneurship
—Investing in Real Estate as a Business

Don't forget your family members and friends that could also benefit from reading this book! A gift like this could change and improve someone's life!

We would love to get your feedback. Let us know how this book has helped you!
What are your thoughts on our other resources? Send your feedback to: info@ShannaMcFarlane.com

Shanna Mcfarlane

Committed to Success

Writing Resource

I fully **commit** to Leveraging my Fear to Achieve my Success!
My Goals/Objectives are:

_____

_____

_____

_____

_____

_____

_____

_____

_____

_____

_____

_____

_____

_____

_____

_____

_____

_____

_____

_____

Writing Resource

Writing Resource

Writing Resource

Writing Resource

_____

_____

_____

_____

_____

_____

_____

_____

_____

_____

_____

_____

_____

_____

_____

_____

_____

_____

_____

_____

_____

_____

_____

_____

Writing Resource

_____

_____

_____

_____

_____

_____

_____

_____

_____

_____

_____

_____

_____

_____

_____

_____

_____

_____

_____

_____

Writing Resource